DEDICATION

This book is dedicated
To my parents, Pleas & Maybelline Sturdivant – who taught me from my childhood
about Jesus Christ

To my mentor and father in the faith, Elijah S. Valley – for lending me your wisdom
for so many years

To my beautiful wife, Jennifer – you are irreplaceably the girl of my dreams
To my baby girl, Nina – My favorite little girl

To my wonderful son, Samuel – for whom this book was written

.

CONTENTS

Corey Sturdivant is one of the most brilliant thinkers of our time. He is an innovative empowerment specialist who works with ministry and corporate executives to develop strategic leadership training, growth & expansion initiatives, vision implementation and so much more. Now, to add to his prodigious list of accomplishments he is the author of this provocative book God Chasers and Iron Men. This book is "must read" for all men, young and old, Christian and Non-Christian alike. It is more than a book, it is a life class. Sturdivant uses his well-rounded perspective of life; coupled with sound biblical teaching to inspire, motivate and challenge the reader to become the person God originally intended him to be. Worthy Challenge #4 is one my favorites: "Let the Past Be the Past." He challenges the reader not to allow past hurts and offenses to continue to ruin or even destroy his life through an unforgiving heart. This entire book is filled with similar challenges motivated by the compassion of God. If you only read one book this year...you have found it here. Read it! You won't regret it!

- Dr. Derrick Traylor

God Chasers
&
Iron Men

COREY D. STURDIVANT

ACKNOWLEDGMENTS

The Men's Group at Goodness & Mercy Outreach Church was gracious enough to test the effectiveness of the Worthy Challenges and I am more than grateful.

FOREWORD
by Rodney D. Hall, PhD.

While the devastating effects of Father-deficient homes are energetically lamented, there remains inadequate force to reverse the trend. Many men, lacking positive and effective role-models, suffer from incomplete identities and lack of purpose. In response, many women have, long-ago, given-up on their dream marriage and have relented to - as if unavoidable - the improper and unhealthy behavior of their partners. Women's strong and tenacious nature allows them to somehow pick up the pieces and make things work. Though highly admirable, this further removes the social expectation of men to conduct their lives with character and integrity. Lacking this expectation, men are further tossed without purpose on the tumultuous cultural ocean where the moral laws of the universe seem to have been replaced with the Experience-Du jure. Worse yet, this cannibalistic cycle feeds an ever-increasing soul-deficiency in both individuals and future generations.

As a longtime Leadership Coach, I have, time-and-again, witnessed the effect of this fatherless cycle in the lives of both men and women. More often than not, these otherwise successful leaders, intuitively recognize that there is something missing in their life. The challenge is that they lack the context and awareness to identify and correct. Although I am usually hired to help my clients develop strategies for greater success, a wonderful bonus benefit often evolves whereby clients are able to turn things around, not only for themselves, but also for their children.

In *God Chasers and Iron Men*, my friend Corey Sturdivant has tapped into several keys and methods that - if applied - will help you transform your life from where you are, back into the image that God had in mind when He created you. Corey has crafted a simple, yet eloquent and authentic, guide that can be enjoyed alone or in a team setting. It can be self-directed by the reader, or can be leader facilitated with a small group. The book serves as a kind of virtual coach, telling true stories and asking significant questions that will probe your mind and reveal your heart. Once you are enlightened, the book provides "Worthy Challenges" to help you shift habits and behaviors to ones that will help you better succeed in all areas of life. I strongly encourage men to not only read this book, but to engage it at every level, reflecting and acting upon its wisdom.

So how do we reverse the trend and create a new generation of men who are great fathers and leaders? We do it one man at a time. Men like you, who will allow God to transform their own life and become role-models for others. I know of no better place to start than *God Chasers and Iron Men*. Enjoy the journey.

Rodney D. Hall, PhD
Certified Life-forming Leadership Coach & Trainer

INTRODUCTION
by Bishop Elijah S. Valley

Earlier this year, I attended my high school's 35th year class reunion. During that weekend, some of my classmates reminded me of comments I made when I ran for class president. As one of the shortest persons in my class, I closed my campaign speech by saying, "remember, dynamite comes in small packages!" This book reminds me of those words. While this book can be a "quick read", it will prove to be a stick of dynamite in the minds of those who will methodically walk through it. Most men can read the entire book in less than an hour. However, it will take weeks, months or years for most men to apply the principles on these pages.

God Chasers and Iron Men isn't just good theory, it is practical advice and "worthy challenges" for any man who wants to fulfill his God given assignment. While society at large is discussing who will be the first woman to become President of The United States, many in Christian circles are debating and discussing the role of women within the Christian community. Unfortunately, I do not believe those debates and discussion will end anytime soon. However, when I hear these discussions, I often wonder if the debates would be as intense if more men would simply stand up and be counted.

As you read about Fran, buying cleats, giving your cell phone a break and offence, you will be challenged to stand up and be counted! The greatest thing about self-assessment is no one gets to see the findings but you. However, in this case, many will see the results as you start to overcome the hurdles in your life that have prevented you from developing godly character.

In the ninth chapter of the Gospel of John, a father and mother were asked how their once blind son received his sight. They replied "he is of age; ask him: he shall speak for himself!" The phrase "of age" speaks of maturity. My beloved Son, Corey Sturdivant, is "of age" and can definitely speak for himself! He speaks from personal experience on every page. It has been my joy and privilege to watch this man of God overcome the "worthy challenges" he penned on these pages!

As you board subways in London, the announcer says, "mind the gap!" Her announcement causes you to pay attention to the space between the platform and the trains' floor. While this generally isn't an enormous space, a misstep could have deadly consequences. God Chasers and Iron Men will challenge you to "mind the gap" between where you are and where you should be. In the words of Michael Buffer, "let's get ready to rumble!"

About 'God Chasers & Iron Men'

God Chasers & Iron Men was written from a father's heart to his son. After years of military service and investigating child and elderly abuse cases, Corey D. Sturdivant understands the realities of absentee fathers and the effects it may have on sons.

The twenty-four worthy challenges in this book are lessons from Sturdivant's heart that he wanted to ensure his son understood and practiced his entire life. God Chasers & Iron Men is designed to foster godly character that benefits all of humanity. Every man should have a copy of this book. If you are up to the challenge, you can be part of a movement that has the potential to change the world for the better.

Each Worthy Challenge is designed to help the reader to develop habits that reflect godly character in stages over 48 months to a year. Each challenge taken should be reviewed after one week using the worthy challenge review. The following week should be used to challenge you to do better in the second week than you did in the first week before moving to the next Worthy Challenge. Are you up for the challenge?

Worthy Challenge #1: Always Keep God First
"You must not have any other god but me."

Exodus 20:3

Decisions! Everyone has to make them. Some are small and may seem unimportant while other decisions are major and have tremendous consequences. Think about it. Throughout your entire life you have had to choose to behave or disobey, to play sports or to join the band, to abuse drugs or to stay clean, to get a job or to go to college, to get married or to remained single, to chase money, clothes, women, houses, cars and titles, or to worship God alone.

Today's "Worthy Challenge" is all about recognizing this one single truth: Anything in our lives that we make more important than God becomes an idol god to us. It is so important to realize this truth because we all want to be successful. We want nice clothes and cars. We want pretty wives and smart and healthy children. We want to make good money and enjoy life. But we must also keep in mind that all of those things are temporary. Jesus once asked, "What good is it for someone to gain the whole world, yet forfeit their soul?" (Mar 8:36).

His point was simple: The most important relationship that any man can have is between he and his maker. Believe me when I say this – God was serious when he said, "You must not have any other gods but me!" We create other gods when we make our decisions based on anything other than pleasing Yahweh. Here are five things that may help you realize who or what you may be worshipping other than God:

1. What do you think about the most?
2. What do you turn to when you feel stressed?
3. What do you spend most of your free-time doing?
4. Who do you talk to about your problems?
5. Who do you talk to the most?

After looking over the list you may be surprised to find out that you've been worshipping money or your spouse. You may even find out that you've been worshipping education or even sex! If so, life is not over. Decide now that this is the day where you turn your heart back to the One, True Living God!

Do This: Before doing or saying anything, ask yourself, "Does this please God?" **Respond accordingly!**

Pray this: Father, I know that you love me because you gave your very best, Jesus Christ to die on the cross for my sins. If you could give your very best for me, the least I can do is return the favor by giving my best to you. You are my God and I vow from this day forward to denounce every other god or idol and worship you with my whole heart. I thank you for hearing my prayer and receiving me as your own. In Jesus' name, Amen.

Worthy Challenge Review

1. On a scale of 1 to 5, 1 being the worst and 5 being the best you could do, how well would you rate your success with this week's worthy challenge?

2. What was your biggest hurdle to overcome as it relates to this week's worthy challenge?

3. What did you do to overcome that hurdle?

4. As you continue into the second week of this challenge, what will you do better than you did last week?

5. On a scale of 1 to 5, 1 being utter failure and 5 being total victory, how successful do you believe you will be as you complete this worthy challenge by the end of this week?

Worthy Challenge #2: Read Your Bible Daily
"I have hidden your word in my heart, that I might not sin against you."

Psalms 119:11

Let's be honest. Some habits are hard to break. This is especially true for routines that have been a part of our lives for years. Just think about your morning routine. If you're like me, you wake up with an angry face and force out a "good morning" grunt to your beautiful wife who is halfway dressed but just as tired as you. Slowly, you sit up on the edge of your bed and push the dogs out of your face – they are so happy to see you this morning. You look at the clock and dread your wakening because you know the tasks that await you at the office.

You stumble into the bathroom in near zombie mode to handle your man business and then brush your teeth angrily before the mirrored sink. After realizing you've been brushing your tongue for 10 minutes, you shake off the remainder of your sleep and the rest of your morning is a rush. You only have fifteen minutes left to get dressed. Your source of news is playing on television as you rush to make some coffee, eat breakfast, kiss the family and head out the door. Halfway to work you realize you left your coffee on the counter and the lunch your wife packed for you is still in the fridge. Darn it! You forgot your suit again. You've been meaning to get dry-cleaned!

Does that sound like your typical morning? No prayer. No daily bread. No meditation. Oh crappy day! Look out world. Here comes my wrath. The following statement is attributed to Albert Einstein: "Insanity is doing the same thing over and over again, expecting different results".

Isaiah 26:3 You will keep in perfect peace all who trust in you, all whose thoughts are fixed on you!

I want to challenge you to change the way you begin your day. Instead of meditating on your work load first thing in the morning, keep a bible on your nightstand. Make it the first thing you reach for in the morning. Find yourself meditating on the Word of God instead of the news reports. The truth is, most of the news reported in mass media is bad news. Car wrecks, late night shootings, natural disasters and celebrity gossip put us in bad moods as soon as the day begins. Break the old habits of kicking the dogs and cursing the song birds.

Do this: Get out of bed early enough to spend at least 15 minutes reading your Bible. Meditate on that passage all day long and apply its principles throughout your day. Try to memorize at least one verse!

Pray this: Father, thank you for your word. I realize old habits are hard to break but with your help, I can replace them with good ones. Give me a heart that yearns for Your Word! I pray this in Jesus' name. Amen!

Worthy Challenge Review

1. On a scale of 1 to 5, 1 being the worst and 5 being the best you could do, how well would you rate your success with this week's worthy challenge?

2. What was your biggest hurdle to overcome as it relates to this week's worthy challenge?

3. What did you do to overcome that hurdle?

4. As you continue into the second week of this challenge, what will you do better than you did last week?

5. On a scale of 1 to 5, 1 being utter failure and 5 being total victory, how successful do you believe you will be as you complete this worthy challenge by the end of this week?

Worthy Challenge #3: Treat People the Way You'd like to be Treated

"Love your neighbor as yourself."

Matthew 22:37

Every day I use the public transit system as part of my commute to and from work. On that bus rides an elderly lady whom I will call "Fran". Fran sits alone and usually sleeps or reads a book for the duration of the ride. One day Fran sat next to a woman who quickly packed her items and changed seats. A few days later as Fran boarded the bus, people (adults) began spraying air fresheners and perfumes in the air. They snickered and sneered as she passed by while others put their personal items in the empty seats next to them to keep her from sitting down.

Fran looked right at me and I greeted her with a smile and said, "Good morning!" She asked if she could sit next to me and I replied, "Sure!" When she sat down we exchanged small talk. I could not ignore the strong smell of urine and some other unidentifiable scent but I refused to treat her the way I saw the others on that bus treat her. I believe Fran feels accepted sitting next to me because since that day, if there is an empty seat next to me Fran will find it and rest easy knowing that she won't be shunned or made fun of.

Did you know that sin stinks to God? In Biblical times, before a priest could go into the Most Holy Place to make atonement on the mercy seat they were required to bathe, change their clothing, and burn incense. The odor of sin was so offensive that God would strike dead anyone who did not complete the ritual before approaching him. This all changed 2000 years ago when Jesus made the ultimate sacrifice to cleanse us thoroughly from the stench of sin. Aren't you glad He didn't run from you when you took your place at his feet?

Is it easy sitting next to Fran? Frankly, no it is not. I don't know if Fran is aware of her own odor. I'm told it has been brought to her attention. What to do about it? I don't know. But what I do know is that I will continue to be kind to Fran and show her the same acceptance and love that Jesus has shown to me. Indeed, if I had an issue, this is how I would want to be treated.

Do this: Whenever you encounter someone who is offensive, determine to love them beyond the offense, just as Christ did for you and for me. Remember to treat them with dignity and respect! After all, they too were created in the image and likeness of God!

Pray this: Jesus, I thank you for receiving me just as I was. Your love for me has taught me how I should treat others. Help me to honor you by receiving your children, despite their shortcomings in order to love them into your Kingdom.

Worthy Challenge Review

1. On a scale of 1 to 5, 1 being the worst and 5 being the best you could do, how well would you rate your success with this week's worthy challenge?

2. What was your biggest hurdle to overcome as it relates to this week's worthy challenge?

3. What did you do to overcome that hurdle?

4. As you continue into the second week of this challenge, what will you do better than you did last week?

5. On a scale of 1 to 5, 1 being utter failure and 5 being total victory, how successful do you believe you will be as you complete this worthy challenge by the end of this week?

Worthy Challenge #4: Let the Past Be the Past

"And forgive us our sins, as we have forgiven those who sin against us."

Matthew 6:12

"You mad, bro?" That question is usually loaded with sarcasm because it is not asked out of genuine concern, nor is it an attempt to rectify relational tensions. To be sure, to ask "You mad, bro?" is simply an attempt to push an agitated individual into rage. The inquisitor is simply pushing emotional buttons. The intent is to provoke, aggravate, and ignite an irrational response to external stimuli, commonly known as offense.

We've all been offended at some point. Think of the man who was abandoned by his father as a boy or the young lady who was sexually molested by her uncle. Imagine the man who feels rejected after discovering an affair between his wife and his best friend. Many of us would consider these transgressions to be unforgiveable – unworthy of grace or mercy. Yet, Jesus challenges our perspective and commands us to view such offense through his eyes.

The Lord's words in the verse above are loaded with significant principles. I recommend you read the chapter in full for a deeper study. For now, let me direct your attention to a few follow-up verses that deal with this week's challenge.

Matthew 6:14-15 continues… "If you forgive those who sin against you, your heavenly Father will forgive you. But if you refuse to forgive others, your Father will not forgive your sins."

Did you catch that? Your capacity to be forgiven is directly proportionate to your willingness to forgive others! There is another scripture that illustrates this powerful principle. **2 Corinthians 9:6 "Remember this: Whoever sows sparingly will also reap sparingly, and whoever sows generously will also reap generously."** We normally only quote this verse when the collection plate is being passed around at church but in reality it's about much more than money. We have to let the past be the past! For your own good – let it go!

Do This: If you have been holding offense towards someone that has asked your forgiveness, let them know that you forgive them and quickly release them from the past. If you need to ask someone for forgiveness, do it this week with a humble spirit.

Pray This: Heavenly Father, I admit that I've been holding on to this offense far too long. I realize that my unwillingness to forgive (<u>Fill in Name:</u> _____) is hindering my relationship with you. I recognize forgiveness is a choice and I choose to let the past be the past today. I believe that you can heal me from the scars and pain I feel from that situation and I receive that healing today. Thank you for forgiving me as I forgive others. In Jesus' name, Amen!

Worthy Challenge Review

1. On a scale of 1 to 5, 1 being the worst and 5 being the best you could do, how well would you rate your success with this week's worthy challenge?

2. What was your biggest hurdle to overcome as it relates to this week's worthy challenge?

3. What did you do to overcome that hurdle?

4. As you continue into the second week of this challenge, what will you do better than you did last week?

5. On a scale of 1 to 5, 1 being utter failure and 5 being total victory, how successful do you believe you will be as you complete this worthy challenge by the end of this week?

Worthy Challenge #5: Be Grateful

"I know what it is to be in need, and I know what it is to have plenty. I have learned the secret of being content in any and every situation, whether well fed or hungry, whether living in plenty or in want."

Philippians 4:12

He knew the day he met her that she would someday be his wife. They became best friends and three years later, they married and moved to Europe. They were dually employed and had no children. Debt free, they traveled as freely as they wanted and rarely ever had reason or need to balance their checkbooks or worry about their bank accounts. They went to a great church, wore nice clothes, and drove beautiful cars. To say life was grand for these love birds is more than an understatement! The favor of the Lord was definitely upon them.

A few years later, after purchasing two homes and birthing two babies, they agreed to move to his hometown in Tennessee. Neither of them had a job lined up and had difficulty finding work so they took a trip to her hometown in Denver, Co. The trip was cut short by news that the puppy they left in the care of a friend had passed away tragically. Things became worse before they got better but they knew in their hearts that God's hand was still upon them and they remained faithful, trusting that God was still in control. Eventually, God restored all and their latter blessings are greater than their past. Though they are young and have plenty more to experience, they can say like Paul, "I know what is to be in need, and I know what it is to have plenty..." Most importantly, they learned how to be content in any given situation.

The story above is very real. It is my personal testimony. This week's worthy challenge is my encouragement to you. As you journey through life, you will have both good times and bad. Some days you can't help but praise God and other days you may question if God is still there on your behalf. I know people who gave up on God when things got tough. They stopped believing that God was in control, or that he cared, or even existed at all. Don't let that be you. Take on the mind of Paul who wrote, **"Yet what we suffer now is nothing compared to the glory he will reveal to us later." (Romans 8:18).**

Do This: Give God thanks daily for the things that you do have. Whenever you feel tempted to envy, give God even more praise for the blessings you currently experience.

Pray this: Father, you have been gracious towards me. You have provided my every need. I know that there are times when I've doubted your love for me and I repent of the sins I committed – the sin of unbelief. You are the sustainer of my life. Help me to honor you at all times in my thoughts, words, and deeds. In Jesus' name, Amen!

Worthy Challenge Review

1. On a scale of 1 to 5, 1 being the worst and 5 being the best you could do, how well would you rate your success with this week's worthy challenge?

2. What was your biggest hurdle to overcome as it relates to this week's worthy challenge?

3. What did you do to overcome that hurdle?

4. As you continue into the second week of this challenge, what will you do better than you did last week?

5. On a scale of 1 to 5, 1 being utter failure and 5 being total victory, how successful do you believe you will be as you complete this worthy challenge by the end of this week?

Worthy Challenge #6: Celebrate Someone Else's Success

"A friend loves at all times, and a brother is born for a time of adversity."

Proverbs 17:17

Most of us know from our childhood the story of the young shepherd boy, David who killed a Philistine giant named Goliath with a rock and a sling shot. Prince Jonathan gave David his gear and King Saul promotes him to Secretary of Defense. They beat down a couple more Philistines on their way home and as the band plays, the cheerleaders change the lyrics to the victory song: **"Saul hath slain his thousands, and David his ten thousands." (1 Samuel 18:7).**

The verse after that tells us that Saul immediately became a hater! What's up with that? Insecure much? Saul was the epitome of insecure. He spends the rest of his years eyeballing David and eventually he made several attempts to kill him. Read 1 Sam 18 for the full story and discover for yourself if you've been acting like a Saul or know someone who is!

It's easy to judge Saul but let's be honest. There have been times in our lives that we've witnessed others get the praise that we think we deserve. Even if we don't deserve the praise, we at times may envy the benefits others enjoy. You've been with the organization for some time and you were the go-to-guy and now, here comes this young college kid – still wet behind the ears. Everyone is acting like he's the best thing since sliced bread and cable television. How do you feel? You mad bro? (See Worthy Challenge #4).

Theologians reading this challenge will quickly point out the fact that God had already informed Saul that he was being stripped from his throne. The prophet Samuel had already anointed David as the next King of Israel and the hearts of the people were turned toward David. So what could Saul have done in light of the fact that such a transition was eminent? The following will determine your legacy – what people remember about you most!

1. Appreciate their contribution to the Kingdom
2. Mentor them as they develop their gifts
3. Support them in tough times
4. Celebrate their success

Do This: Find a young man that has potential for greatness at work or at church and begin to mentor them. Encourage, correct, and instruct them as Jesus did with his disciples.

Pray This: Dear Lord, you have blessed me in more ways than I can count. Help me to be a blessing to someone else.   Connect me to someone who has the ability and heart to advance the Kingdom of Heaven for your name sake. I humbly submit my gifts back to you. In Jesus' name, Amen!

Worthy Challenge Review

1. On a scale of 1 to 5, 1 being the worst and 5 being the best you could do, how well would you rate your success with this week's worthy challenge?

2. What was your biggest hurdle to overcome as it relates to this week's worthy challenge?

3. What did you do to overcome that hurdle?

4. As you continue into the second week of this challenge, what will you do better than you did last week?

5. On a scale of 1 to 5, 1 being utter failure and 5 being total victory, how successful do you believe you will be as you complete this worthy challenge by the end of this week?

Worthy Challenge #7: Take Time to Rest

"On the seventh day God had finished his work of creation, so he rested from all his work."

Genesis 2:2

"Okay, let me get this right. The creator of Heaven and Earth and everything else that exists finds time to rest but you're too busy to take a time-out? You've got to be kidding me!" Those are the words I said to myself after a near mental breakdown. Thank God I recovered, but only after I repented. "Repented" may be at first glance an odd choice of words to you, but that's exactly what many of us need to do in order to get out of the crazy cycle of busyness that leaves us feeling worn down and unsatisfied by the week's end.

According to Genesis 1:26 we are all made in the "image and likeness" of God. If this is the case, then why don't we schedule time to rest? Think about it. After a week of productive work, God took an entire day to rest. We, on the other hand, go from one finished product or job to the next. Seamlessly, we pick up more work without even taking the time to appreciate what we have already accomplished. We go from high school straight to college – from college to the work force – and from one job to the next. That is why we need to repent. Our lifestyles are not representing the image and the likeness of the Creator.

Let's move over into the New Testament and meditate on the words Jesus chose to exhort us to rest.

"Come to me, all you who are weary and burdened, and I will give you rest. Take my yoke upon you and learn from me, for I am gentle and humble in heart, and you will find rest for your souls. For my yoke is easy and my burden is light."

Matthew 11:28-30

Do you see what's happening here? While we are busy trying to work hard for Jesus, He is steady offering us rest. He wants us to represent the Father in every way, and that includes not only satisfying work, but quality rest also.

Do This: Journal how you spend your time daily for a week. At the end of the week, analyze your schedule and eliminate what you can. Block out a time or day of rest for the following week and do that – nothing more. Enjoy your gift of rest and thank God for it!

Pray This: Forgive me, God for not heading to your voice. You have called me to enjoy divine rest in your presence and I instead have taken on unnecessary burdens. I repent of this today and ask that you receive me once again to my right place in you. I'm thankful for the rest that you have offered to me. In Jesus' name, Amen!

Worthy Challenge Review

1. On a scale of 1 to 5, 1 being the worst and 5 being the best you could do, how well would you rate your success with this week's worthy challenge?

2. What was your biggest hurdle to overcome as it relates to this week's worthy challenge?

3. What did you do to overcome that hurdle?

4. As you continue into the second week of this challenge, what will you do better than you did last week?

5. On a scale of 1 to 5, 1 being utter failure and 5 being total victory, how successful do you believe you will be as you complete this worthy challenge by the end of this week?

Worthy Challenge #8: Don't Be Greedy – Share Your Faith

"Therefore go and make disciples of all nations, baptizing them in the name of the Father and of the Son and of the Holy Spirit, and teaching them to obey everything I have commanded you...

Matthew 28:19-20

Perhaps no other scripture defines Christianity more precise than Matthew 28:19. Still, there are many people who claim to be Christians that will not, under any circumstances, share their faith. We've heard every excuse in the book from, "I don't know enough" to "I evangelize by my lifestyle". Do any of these excuses ring a bell? Personally, I've been guilty of using both of them early in my Christian walk. I realize now that the real reason I did not share my faith was because I feared that I would not know what to say – fear that I would look like a religious fanatic – fear that I would fail!

Think back to the day you decided to receive Jesus as your personal Savior. That person that shared their faith with you or invited you to church probably was not some theology professor or dean of Apologetics at the local Christian College. If the statistic is correct, the person who led you to Christ was more than likely a friend or family member who simply loved you enough to share their own personal testimony with you. Their witness of our Lord's saving grace is evidence of the power of God within them.

For I am not ashamed of the gospel, because it is the power of God that brings salvation to everyone who believes... (Romans 1:16)

What a relief! That's great news! Why? Because what this means for us is that we don't have to be afraid to fail since it is the power of God that converts sinners. The only thing God expects from us is that we be obedient to the Great Commission (Mat 28:19-20). Once we do that, He will take care of the rest. Think of it as a team effort. With God on our side, there's no way we can lose!

Do This: Write out your personal testimony and practice telling it in the mirror. Pray over it and thank God for the person(s) who shared their testimony with you. Before the week is out, share your testimony with someone you know that has not received Jesus Christ in their hearts. Be sure to share with love and leave the rest to God.

Pray This: Heavenly Father, for too long I have made excuses as to why I don't share my faith. This ends today. Your word gives me confidence in knowing that you only require my obedience to share while your Holy Spirit does the work of conversion. I ask you now for Holy boldness as I seek to make disciples in your name. In Jesus' name, Amen.

Worthy Challenge Review

1. On a scale of 1 to 5, 1 being the worst and 5 being the best you could do, how well would you rate your success with this week's worthy challenge?

2. What was your biggest hurdle to overcome as it relates to this week's worthy challenge?

3. What did you do to overcome that hurdle?

4. As you continue into the second week of this challenge, what will you do better than you did last week?

5. On a scale of 1 to 5, 1 being utter failure and 5 being total victory, how successful do you believe you will be as you complete this worthy challenge by the end of this week?

Worthy Challenge #9: Forgive Yourself

"When they had finished eating, Jesus said to Simon Peter, "Simon son of John, do you love me more than these?" "Yes, Lord," he said, "you know that I love you." Jesus said, "Feed my lambs."

John 21:15

When I was a kid a friend of mine had a secret he wanted to tell a group of guys that I hung out with. When I approached to hear the secret he said, "Not you man, you're a church boy". I quickly responded, "I ain't no church boy!" The look he gave me was the first demonic expression that I ever saw. It frightened me. He didn't say a single word but waved me in to hear the secret. My heart was troubled because at age 12, I had denied the Christ!

The text you just read captures a discussion between Jesus and Simon (also known as Peter) shortly after His resurrection. To be sure, this interaction is only days after Peter denied – not once, not twice, but three times – his relationship with Jesus! Let's not be so judgmental about Peter; however, because I want you to know that there is a bit of Simon-Peter in all of us. Yes. One day we love the Lord more than anything and the next day we deny any association with Him.

We deny our relationship with Christ whenever we sin. How do I know? Because Jesus said, "Anyone who loves me will obey my teaching. My Father will love them, and we will come to them and make our home with them. Anyone who does not love me will not obey my teaching. These words you hear are not my own; they belong to the Father who sent me." (John 14:23-24)

The great news is that although we may fall short sometimes, God's grace often leaves room for repentance. Just like Peter, we can recover! We can get back on the right track and receive God's grace and mercy. The important thing to understand here is that our forgiveness, our righteousness in Christ, Jesus is not based on how we feel but on the promises of God's word that has declared that he is just and faithful to forgive. He forgave Peter. He forgave me; and He will forgive you too.

Do This: Whenever someone tries to make you feel guilty for past sins, failures or mistakes tell them "God has forgiven me for that and I have forgiven myself." Wake up every morning with a fresh mind – free from yesterday's mistakes, knowing that you have been forgiven and thus you can forgive yourself, too.

Pray This: Oh God, your word promised in 1 John 1:9 that you are faithful and just to forgive our sins. I realize that my sins have been an expression of denial that I am a child of the Living God. Please restore me back into relationship with you. Thank you for loving me in spite of my sins. Give me the strength to do what is right in the face of adversity. In Jesus' name, Amen.

Worthy Challenge Review

1. On a scale of 1 to 5, 1 being the worst and 5 being the best you could do, how well would you rate your success with this week's worthy challenge?

2. What was your biggest hurdle to overcome as it relates to this week's worthy challenge?

3. What did you do to overcome that hurdle?

4. As you continue into the second week of this challenge, what will you do better than you did last week?

5. On a scale of 1 to 5, 1 being utter failure and 5 being total victory, how successful do you believe you will be as you complete this worthy challenge by the end of this week?

Worthy Challenge #10: Avoid Counter-Productive Conversation

"Don't use foul or abusive language. Let everything you say be good and helpful, so that your words will be an encouragement to those who hear them."

Ephesians 4:29

The United States military is one of the most eclectic organizations on the planet. Take at random fifty men – farmers, attorneys, electricians, black, white, Hispanic, rich and poor and make them share confined space for a few weeks and something is bound to happen. Someone is going to be offended or misunderstood. In most cases, it is what was said that caused the fight – a negative comment that triggered an emotional response. The statement may have even been true, but the question is "was it productive?"

Each day yields the potential for us to offend or become offended. We can speak truth and be offensive. But we can also speak truth and be appreciated. My mentor, Bishop Elijah S. Valley has the ability to talk almost anyone into nearly anything. We once took a large group to see a Gospel artist perform and the place was overbooked. Security blocked the doors and we watched them turn hundreds of people away. Bishop Valley walked up to the security guard and after about 90 seconds of interaction, the guard opened the doors to allow 25 strangers inside the already overcrowded arena. When I asked him how he was able to get us in he replied, "You can catch more flies with honey than with vinegar". Can you remember a time when your words destroyed a relationship? If you could do it over what would you say different?

If it is possible, as far as it depends on you, live at peace with everyone

(Romans 12:18)

Do This: In every conversation this week, before you say anything, take time to think about the words you plan to use. Then ask yourself if those words are good, helpful, and encouraging to the person who hears them. If not, keep them to yourself. Control your thoughts and you can control your tongue.

Pray This: Father I ask you to forgive me for any pain that my words have caused in my neighbor's life. I know that my words can build others up or destroy them. Destructive conversation, gossip, abusive language, and

dirty jokes are not fruitful and should not be a part of my life. Thank you for bringing this to my attention. Let now my words be used only for the benefit of others and the building up of your Kingdom! In Jesus' name, Amen.

Worthy Challenge Review

1. On a scale of 1 to 5, 1 being the worst and 5 being the best you could do, how well would you rate your success with this week's worthy challenge?

2. What was your biggest hurdle to overcome as it relates to this week's worthy challenge?

3. What did you do to overcome that hurdle?

4. As you continue into the second week of this challenge, what will you do better than you did last week?

5. On a scale of 1 to 5, 1 being utter failure and 5 being total victory, how successful do you believe you will be as you complete this worthy challenge by the end of this week?

Worthy Challenge #11: Celebrate Your Own Success
"God saw all that he had made, and it was very good..."

Genesis 1:31

My family loves football season. I played football growing up. I live in the south so you should know that we are serious about our football. My son plays pee-wee football and is remarkably great at defense. Believe me – I'm not just saying that because he's my son. I once watched proudly as he took down a blocker and the ball carrier with one powerful tackle. The sideline cheered him on tremendously but this praise hardly fazed my son. After he made the play, he got off the turf, dusted himself off and got in position as he awaited the next play. I told my wife, if that were me I would have trash-talked for the rest of the game! That guy would have never forgotten my number!

That may sound arrogant to some of you who are graced to walk in divine humility. But even the humble should take time to reflect on their great work and smile upon their accomplishments. I don't mean that one should carry an attitude of conceit but I believe that God gives us moments in life where we can appreciate the gifts, talents, and abilities that He has given us. The psalmist wrote in Psalm 139:14, **"I praise you because I am fearfully and wonderfully made; your works are wonderful, I know that full well."** What kind of success do you suppose the author experienced to make such a bold declaration? Was it a great battle won? The previous verses give us a clue. Read them and you will find that whatever he was going through, he was sure that God was always with him. That very fact is the reason why we can celebrate success. Our boasting is in the truth that God is on our side and He promised to never leave or forsake us!

I intentionally talk to my son after his games about the good things he did out on the field. I want him to celebrate those successful events because as he goes through life, most people will only point out his flaws. King David understood that there are times when you will have to encourage yourself. That's when the testimony of past success is to the utmost importance.

Do This: Take time to celebrate the things God has blessed you to excel in. The next time you hit a good ball, bask in the moment. When you receive a bonus or a promotion on your job, praise God for your innovative talent. When you do something well, acknowledge that it was good.

Pray This: Thank you, Lord for making me the way you have. You created me in a marvelous way to do wonderful things. I am created in your image and likeness. Because of this, I am destined for greatness! Let everything I do bring your name glory. In Jesus' name, Amen.

Worthy Challenge Review

1. On a scale of 1 to 5, 1 being the worst and 5 being the best you could do, how well would you rate your success with this week's worthy challenge?

2. What was your biggest hurdle to overcome as it relates to this week's worthy challenge?

3. What did you do to overcome that hurdle?

4. As you continue into the second week of this challenge, what will you do better than you did last week?

5. On a scale of 1 to 5, 1 being utter failure and 5 being total victory, how successful do you believe you will be as you complete this worthy challenge by the end of this week?

Worthy Challenge #12: Work Hard to Perfect Your Craft

"Teach me knowledge and good judgment, for I trust your commands."

Psa 119:66

Teaching is my passion. For me, there is almost nothing as rewarding as sharing information that impacts a learner's life. I have coached football, taught high school students, and educated military members and their families on a plethora of issues. I regularly teach and lead a small men's group. It is in my nature to look for teachable moments when I'm with my children as I take childrearing seriously.

Although I love to teach, nothing annoys me more than a know-it-all. There are some people that you can't tell anything. You know the type. They are right in the middle of doing something dead wrong and when you correct them they respond with, "I know." Well, if you know that already then why are you doing it wrong? People like this are un-teachable and will, in most cases have to learn almost everything the hard way – by failing! Perfecting your craft takes time, discipline, and constructive criticism. But the chief elements are a teachable spirit and a humble heart. Proverbs 2:1-5 gives a simple model for learning:

> **My son, if you accept my words and store up my commands within you, turning your ear to wisdom and applying your heart to understanding— indeed, if you call out for insight and cry aloud for understanding, and if you look for it as for silver and search for it as for hidden treasure, then you will understand the fear of the LORD and find the knowledge of God.**

What this means for us is that our learning must be intentional. We are called to look beyond the wisdom of man and seek the wisdom of God. To be sure, teachers are the tools God uses to pass along knowledge. The Holy Spirit illuminates that knowledge and gives us the power to make something great of it. Romans 12:5-8 encourages us to be good stewards with our gifts, practicing as often as possible to prove we are part of the Body of Christ. Whatever gift God has blessed you with, perfect it for His glory.

Do This: Whenever you have an opportunity to exercise your gift, do it to the best of your ability. If your crowd is small, pretend you are on television in front of millions. Better still; work your gift as if God is the only one watching. Remember, do it all as unto the Lord!

Pray This: Thank you, Holy Spirit for guiding my learning. I want to bring your name glory in all that I do. I pray now for divine wisdom. Show me your ways, Father so that I don't fail. Thank you for teaching me to do well. In Jesus' name, Amen.

Worthy Challenge Review

1. On a scale of 1 to 5, 1 being the worst and 5 being the best you could do, how well would you rate your success with this week's worthy challenge?

2. What was your biggest hurdle to overcome as it relates to this week's worthy challenge?

3. What did you do to overcome that hurdle?

4. As you continue into the second week of this challenge, what will you do better than you did last week?

5. On a scale of 1 to 5, 1 being utter failure and 5 being total victory, how successful do you believe you will be as you complete this worthy challenge by the end of this week?

Worthy Challenge #13: Set Life Goals for Yourself
"Good planning and hard work lead to prosperity, but hasty shortcuts lead to poverty."

Proverbs 21:5

As men, most of us enjoy a certain level of spontaneity. We like to surprise our wives with exotic vacations. We enjoy the sudden knockout punch in a boxing match. The unbeknownst drag race at the traffic light with the stranger in the muscle car sends chills up our spines. We look forward to business trips. Really all we need is a reason to do something different; something exciting! But if we are not careful, we can mistake procrastination for spontaneity. Spontaneity describes an act of impulse, without effort or premeditation. Procrastination is when we put off or delay acting or deciding on something that requires immediate attention. Usually, procrastination is the result of poor planning.

In Steven R. Covey's The 7 Habits of Highly Effective People, he argued, "The key is not to prioritize what's on your schedule, but to schedule your priorities."[1] What's important to understand here is that without a plan everything has the potential to take priority and consequently, one becomes aimless and achieves less.

Study the creation history in Genesis and you will find that even God planned for success. Everything that mankind would need was prepared before man was created. If God had not planned, and made man before the water or vegetation, how long do you suppose would man have lasted? Even into the more intricate details of time, the Lord informed the prophet in Jeremiah 1:5, "Before I formed you I the womb I knew you, before you were born I set you apart; I appointed you as a prophet to the nations." Jeremiah's life was in the plan of God. He would later tell the prophet in Jeremiah 29:11, "For I know the plans I have for you," declares the LORD, "plans to prosper you and not to harm you, plans to give you hope and a future."

Joseph's planning was key to millions of people surviving a desert famine. Solomon's temple was a success because of the plans his father, David left for him. Even our very existence, according to Ephesians 1:11 is a product of the plan of God. Planning is essential to any good thing. Jesus reminds us of this in John 14:3

---

[1] Steven R. Covey, The 7 Habits of Highly effective People. (New York; Free Press. 2004) 161.

"And if I go and prepare a place for you, I will come back and take you to be with me that you also may be where I am."

Do This: Imagine what you want your life to look like in five years and write your vision down in detail. Work backwards in 12 to 18 month increments, creating milestones to accomplish until you get to what you need to do today. Focus your energy on making that plan a reality, adjust when necessary but don't give up on your dream.

Pray This: Lord, I know you have a plan for my life. I pray as I write out my goals that your Spirit would guide me down the path you have already prepared for me. I want to be in your will. Give me what to desire and I will follow hard after you. Thank you for direction. In Jesus' name, Amen.

Worthy Challenge Review

1. On a scale of 1 to 5, 1 being the worst and 5 being the best you could do, how well would you rate your success with this week's worthy challenge?

2. What was your biggest hurdle to overcome as it relates to this week's worthy challenge?

3. What did you do to overcome that hurdle?

4. As you continue into the second week of this challenge, what will you do better than you did last week?

5. On a scale of 1 to 5, 1 being utter failure and 5 being total victory, how successful do you believe you will be as you complete this worthy challenge by the end of this week?

Worthy Challenge #14: Apologize When You're Wrong

"People who conceal their sins will not prosper, but if they confess and turn from them, they will receive mercy."

Proverbs 28:13

Most of us know at least one person who is too prideful to ever apologize for anything. They could step on your toe and blame you for leaving your foot in that place while they were walking past the couch that you are sitting on. They will never admit to being wrong even when all of the evidence clearly proves that they are. These people don't have many friends because "something is wrong with everybody" except for them. Do you know anyone who fits that description? If you do then pray for them!

My heart ached as I prepared to write this challenge because I have made a lot of mistakes in my life. Because I minister from the perspective of my own personal experience, I could not avoid reflecting on the people that I have hurt and the relationships that I destroyed in the process. I have been able to apologize to some of them. It is in my heart to apologize to others but circumstances do not allow it. Either way, it was imperative that I repent from my old ways. I am now rather quick to apologize and I hope others would treat me likewise.

"Make every effort to live in peace with everyone and to be holy; without holiness no one will see the Lord." (Hebrews 12:14)

Often we hear people say, "I'm over it" after they've had a dispute with someone and have not reconciled the relationship. This is a cop out! Someone is offended because they've been wronged by you and you are over it? You have not apologized or repented but "they just need to grow up and get a life". Does this sound like someone who is sorry for wronging their brother or sister in Christ? What would you say to a person behaving this way in light of the scriptures we just read?

Do This: The next time someone informs you that something you said or did has hurt or offended them listen to them and apologize. If it was a misunderstanding, communicate that without being argumentative. Do what it takes to make peace.

Pray This: Dear Jesus, I know that I am not perfect and at times I may offend others around me. I pray that you would cause me to walk in your wisdom and

help me to do all that is in my power to live peaceably with my family, friends, and even strangers. Humble my heart so that when I am wrong I am not too prideful to ask forgiveness. Thank you for your grace and mercy. For your glory, Amen.

Worthy Challenge Review

1. On a scale of 1 to 5, 1 being the worst and 5 being the best you could do, how well would you rate your success with this week's worthy challenge?

2. What was your biggest hurdle to overcome as it relates to this week's worthy challenge?

3. What did you do to overcome that hurdle?

4. As you continue into the second week of this challenge, what will you do better than you did last week?

5. On a scale of 1 to 5, 1 being utter failure and 5 being total victory, how successful do you believe you will be as you complete this worthy challenge by the end of this week?

Worthy Challenge #15: Choose to Love

"Whoever claims to love God yet hates a brother or sister is a liar. For whoever does not love their brother and sister, whom they have seen, cannot love God, whom they have not seen."

1 John 4:20

I preached a sermon a few years ago about love one Sunday after hearing some disturbing lyrics by a young vocalist who sang, "I don't want to be loved. I just want a quickie." And I thought to myself, "What kind of horrible example of love has this young man experienced that has turned him off to the idea of being loved. In fact, He has chosen not to." Evidently, he's never had real love. Real love makes food taste better. It's that kind of love that makes certain songs memorable. It's what a child feels when the world is cruel; yet Momma knows just the right words to make him feel special.

But like the singer I just mentioned, I wonder how many of us have chosen against love. Like a 3rd grader with a crush, we'd rather kick someone than hug them. After worship service we shoot out the back door like roaches exposed to light. Heaven forbid someone utter those three words: I…Love…You!

On a more serious note, we've justified being selective with whom we show love. For many, your past hurts dictate your present scrutiny. We've allowed mental mapping theories to excuse us from loving difficult people, especially when having to love them makes us uncomfortable. Your love is therefore reserved for family and only if we're lucky enough, we too can become part of your conditional circle of trust. We call it self-preservation; protecting our heart, etc.

You've been hurt before, I get that. And the last person you tried to help took advantage of you. I get that too. But you can't let your scars keep you from living. Jesus declares, **"The thief comes only to steal and kill and destroy; I have come that they may have life, and have it to the full"** (John 10:10). Jesus loves without prejudice or exception! Will you be like Him or will you be like the thief. Love is a choice. Choose wisely.

Do This: Learn to control your thoughts about people who you have found to be difficult to love. Show them you love them by meeting their needs without looking for a "thank you" or anything else. Just love them.

Pray This: Lord, I thank you for loving me enough to sacrifice your life on the cross for me. Help me to love sacrificially so that I can glorify you. Help me to love people who have wronged me. Help me to love all of my neighbors without prejudice or exception. In Jesus' name, Amen!

Worthy Challenge Review

1. On a scale of 1 to 5, 1 being the worst and 5 being the best you could do, how well would you rate your success with this week's worthy challenge?

2. What was your biggest hurdle to overcome as it relates to this week's worthy challenge?

3. What did you do to overcome that hurdle?

4. As you continue into the second week of this challenge, what will you do better than you did last week?

5. On a scale of 1 to 5, 1 being utter failure and 5 being total victory, how successful do you believe you will be as you complete this worthy challenge by the end of this week?

Worthy Challenge #16: Make New Friends

"When I am with those who are weak, I share their weakness, for I want to bring the weak to Christ. Yes, I try to find common ground with everyone, doing everything I can to save some."

1 Corinthians 9:22

I have a confession to make. Other than football, I don't care much for watching televised sports. I love sports. I just become bored watching them without the scent of hotdogs and popcorn. I'd rather sit on hot bleachers and step in spilled mustard than sit in a Lazy-Boy and listen to amateur analysts coach from the comfort of their couch. Yet, I find myself on occasion at the chicken wing place or a neighbor's bar-b-cue watching a game that I don't care about and struggling to stay awake. Why do I do what I do? For the same reason you watch chic-flics with your wife or mother. I do this for the same reason you read pre-school books with your children and play video games with the neighbor's kid. For the same reason you swing golf clubs with your boss and bring doughnuts for your co-workers. We do it in order to build relationships with people we hope to influence. Kenneth O. Gangel believes "It is highly unlikely that effective mentoring could result without a significant friendship between leader and follower."[2] I agree. Apparently the apostle Paul does too. Take a look at the greetings from his letters:

Romans 1:7 "To all who are in Rome, loved by God...Grace to you and peace..."

1 Corinthians 1:4 "I always thank my God for you..."

Ephesians 1:1 "To the faithful saints in Christ Jesus..."

I gather that Paul realized that the secret to building relationships included the ability to encourage others – not from a high horse, but on their level; on common ground. This worthy challenge is not about becoming popular. It's about doing whatever we can to save lost men.

Do This: Eliminate anything that will distract you from making eye-contact with people while in public places. If you're at the gym this week, take off the headphones to send the message that you are available to listen. If you are out shopping, put away your cell phone and say "Hello" to people who pass by. Look

---

[2] Kenneth O. Gangle. *Team Leadership in Christian Ministry.* (Chicago: Moody Publishers, 1997) 262.

for opportunities to engage in conversations that can lead to discussions about their salvation.

Pray This: Father, I have fallen short when it comes to winning souls to Christ. I am eliminating things that avert relationships from being made as I realize that there is a world of people who need Christians to be on high-alert. Send people my way so that I can share the truth of the Gospel with. In Jesus' name, Amen.

Worthy Challenge Review

1. On a scale of 1 to 5, 1 being the worst and 5 being the best you could do, how well would you rate your success with this week's worthy challenge?

2. What was your biggest hurdle to overcome as it relates to this week's worthy challenge?

3. What did you do to overcome that hurdle?

4. As you continue into the second week of this challenge, what will you do better than you did last week?

5. On a scale of 1 to 5, 1 being utter failure and 5 being total victory, how successful do you believe you will be as you complete this worthy challenge by the end of this week?

Worthy Challenge #17: Learn Something New

"Your hands made me and formed me; give me understanding to learn your commands."

Psalms 119:73

While out shopping for cleats with my wife and kids (my son busted through his old pair during a football game), my daughter and I wondered off into the book section. Eventually my wife and my son joined us and we searched with prejudice for literature that would interest us. After a good 45 minutes, I corralled the family and we went to the cashier to make our purchase. In my hand I held my 3 selected books. My daughter required a small buggy to carry hers. My wife and my son emerged empty-handed but he did find an awesome pair of cleats at the next store we visited.

When we got home I sat on the couch and began skimming over my latest treasure while my daughter sprawled out on the living room floor with at least a half-dozen books about horses. "Daddy," she asked, "Which book should I read first?" I looked up and pointed to a random book and she happily began reading it. My wife slowly shook her head and said, "She clearly gets this from you." Proudly I smiled. My daughter – the beautiful nerd!

I love the fact that our youthful generation is hungry for information. According to Barna Group, "younger pastors buy more books per year than do older pastors."[3] With books being easily accessible most of us are without excuse when it comes to gathering new information. Even more, if we are to combat the false doctrines and immoral and perverse philosophies of our worldly counterparts, we must be willing to learn as much as we can. As lifelong students, we should always seek a better understanding of God's commands.

Do This: If you are not a reader, start reading at least one book each month. If you already read, challenge yourself to add another book to your monthly average or began writing book reviews that cause you to think critically about what you are reading.

---

[3] "Reading Habits of Today's Pastors." Barna Group. https://www.barna.org/barna-update/congregations/613-reading-habits-of-today-s-pastors (accessed September 17, 2013).

Pray This: Dear God, I thank you for giving me a mind capable of learning. I realize that there are a lot of things that I don't know but your wisdom is infinite. For the sake of your Kingdom, I will strive to learn all that I can so that I can be ready to give an answer of truth against the false doctrines and teachings of the world. In Jesus' name, Amen.

Worthy Challenge Review

1. On a scale of 1 to 5, 1 being the worst and 5 being the best you could do, how well would you rate your success with this week's worthy challenge?

2. What was your biggest hurdle to overcome as it relates to this week's worthy challenge?

3. What did you do to overcome that hurdle?

4. As you continue into the second week of this challenge, what will you do better than you did last week?

5. On a scale of 1 to 5, 1 being utter failure and 5 being total victory, how successful do you believe you will be as you complete this worthy challenge by the end of this week?

Worthy Challenge #18: Laugh For a Change

"We were filled with laughter, and we sang for joy. And the other nations said, "What amazing things the LORD has done for them."

Psalms 126:2

I once visited a church that made sure I would never return. The experience was so horrible that I am convinced their assignment was to make it clear to me that I was not a welcomed guest. This church had a parking lot ministry that made me find my own place to park. Greeters at the front doors that gave me the prison stare as I walked past them; only tilting their chins slightly to say, "Sup?" in exchange for my, "Good afternoon." Once inside the sanctuary it was every man for himself. I found a seat for me and my family near the back of the church. When the service started, several ladies draped in all white took to the microphones and sang a medley to us with military-like perfection. This was followed up with a brief prayer and a traditional welcome announcement from the church administrator. All of this was accomplished without a single person cracking even the slightest smile. I thought of pulling out my video camera and recording for the sake of creating a short film entitled *Church Zombies*.

During the service I was asked to share an announcement about our upcoming conference. I stood to my feet and attempted to hand the ushers a flyer advertising the event. Reluctantly, they took the flyer but I'm quite certain it was quickly discarded into the fiery furnace that must have been in the basement of this facility they called the House of God! I was certainly glad to leave the service and overly grateful for the joy and peace that seemed to fill our church the following Wednesday night. As the saying goes, "There's no place like home."

If you have read this far and have not cracked a single smile then you are probably a member of that church I'm talking about. No matter how serious you think you are, some things are just funny. I recently read an article that suggested "children laugh as much as 400 times per day" but grumpy, crusty, old adults laugh only 15 times per day on average.[4]

---

[4] Elizabeth Scott. "The Stress Management and Health Benefits of Laughter." about.com. http://stress.about.com/od/stresshealth/a/laughter.htm (accessed September 19, 2013).

Do This: Visit http://stress.about.com/od/stresshealth/a/laughter.htm for the benefits of laughter and utilize at least two of the author's strategies for adding laughter to your life for the next two weeks.

Pray This: Father, I thank you for the joy you have placed in my heart. Your word declares that there is a time for everything. That includes a time to laugh. I believe you desire your people to be happy even while we remain on the earth. I refuse to be bound by anger, frustration, un-forgiveness, or anything else. In Jesus Christ, my joy is complete. Amen!

Worthy Challenge Review

1. On a scale of 1 to 5, 1 being the worst and 5 being the best you could do, how well would you rate your success with this week's worthy challenge?

2. What was your biggest hurdle to overcome as it relates to this week's worthy challenge?

3. What did you do to overcome that hurdle?

4. As you continue into the second week of this challenge, what will you do better than you did last week?

5. On a scale of 1 to 5, 1 being utter failure and 5 being total victory, how successful do you believe you will be as you complete this worthy challenge by the end of this week?

Worthy Challenge #19: Express Your Creativity

"Look!" he said. "The people are united, and they all speak the same language. After this, nothing they set out to do will be impossible for them!"

Genesis 11:6

The passage just read is God's response after observing what people can accomplish when they work together in a spirit of unity. Do not let the fact that their endeavor was evil allow you to miss the principle truth that God created all of us in His image and likeness. It is undoubtedly clear that a major part of God's likeness that we have inherited includes the ability to create at levels far beyond anything other creature on earth. Beavers build dams, hornets construct nests, and spiders weave beautiful webs but none of that compares to the complexity of mega-structures, cathedrals, and technology that mankind has been able to produce.

It bothers me to hear a person say that they have no creativity because such claims suggest that they were made more like a gnat than a man. A man without creativity worries me. I'm afraid he may soon believe that his existence is unnecessary since he contributes nothing to his world, community, family, or home. In reality, we all have creative proclivities. The irony is that those who claim to have none have mastered the ability to stifle their own creativity or ignore their creative urges altogether. To be clear, the seasoned man who keeps his ideas to himself during a brainstorming session, the business man who takes no risks for fear of making a mistake, the batter who won't swing because he may strike out – these people are masters of nothingness. They don't know their own creative power because they refuse to show the world – no; they refuse to even show themselves what they are capable of.

I will praise you because I have been remarkably and wonderfully made. Your works are wonderful, and I know this very well (Psalms 139:14).

Imagine what our world would be like if everyone believed as the psalmist, that God took particular interest in making each of us in a remarkable way. What would you do if you were not afraid to fail? What would you say if you were not afraid of how others would perceive your ideas? How can your gifts and abilities make a difference in the world?

Do This: Memorize Psa. 139:14 and recite it to yourself whenever you have an opportunity to express creativity.

Pray This: Father, for too long I have allowed myself to be limited by the opinions of others, to include my own. I know that you have created me in your image and likeness. This means that there is greatness inside of me. Help me to be fearless. This requires faith. From this day on, I will put my faith in you to accomplish your will in my life. Thank you for equipping me to do a great work. I will do everything unto you. In Jesus' name, Amen!

Worthy Challenge Review

1. On a scale of 1 to 5, 1 being the worst and 5 being the best you could do, how well would you rate your success with this week's worthy challenge?

2. What was your biggest hurdle to overcome as it relates to this week's worthy challenge?

3. What did you do to overcome that hurdle?

4. As you continue into the second week of this challenge, what will you do better than you did last week?

5. On a scale of 1 to 5, 1 being utter failure and 5 being total victory, how successful do you believe you will be as you complete this worthy challenge by the end of this week?

Worthy Challenge #20: Help Without Motives
"Offer hospitality to one another without grumbling."

1 Peter 4:9

My wife is a chef. She has the ability to taste something at a restaurant and recreate it at home with precision. I, on the other hand am what I like to call domestically challenged. Sure, I can handle my business on a grill (serious man points), but don't ask me to prepare some gourmet dish like the famous chef Emeril Lagasse. I leave the serious stuff like Christmas and Thanksgiving dinner to my wife.

The great thing about her ability to cook is that it coincides well with my keenness to entertain house guests. When people come to our home, our goal is to make them feel like it is their home. Most times we don't ask our guest to bring anything with them except for their game-face and a sense of humor. We want them to experience the best meal they've ever had while they laugh and relax, trusting that they can safely let down their guards and just be themselves.

"Then he turned to his host. "When you put on a luncheon or a banquet," he said, "don't invite your friends, brothers, relatives, and rich neighbors. For they will invite you back, and that will be your only reward" (Luke 14:12).

Each of us knows someone who will not do a single thing unless they receive some type of compensation. Let's just be honest. You might even be that person. Heaven forbid you hold the fire extinguisher when Granny's house catches fire. She'd best spit the fire out if she doesn't have a dollar to pay for your help. We may laugh and shake our heads as I exaggerate the story but the behavior is a shameful reality that is often found amongst even Christians. Please, don't let this be said about you.

Do This: Make it a point each week to help at least one person or organization that does not have the means to repay you. Do it with excellence – without grumbling or complaining.

Pray This: Thank you, Lord for blessing me with skills, abilities, and finances to build up your Kingdom. For times that I have been selfish, please forgive me. I realized that you have blessed me to be a blessing and I will no longer take this fact for granted. From this day on, I will give back to you by helping those who

are not able to help themselves, just as you would do. Thank you for being
patient with me. In Jesus' name, Amen!

Worthy Challenge Review

1. On a scale of 1 to 5, 1 being the worst and 5 being the best you could do, how well would you rate your success with this week's worthy challenge?

2. What was your biggest hurdle to overcome as it relates to this week's worthy challenge?

3. What did you do to overcome that hurdle?

4. As you continue into the second week of this challenge, what will you do better than you did last week?

5. On a scale of 1 to 5, 1 being utter failure and 5 being total victory, how successful do you believe you will be as you complete this worthy challenge by the end of this week?

Worthy Challenge #21: Make Every Moment Count

"Be wise in the way you act toward outsiders; make the most of every opportunity."

Colossians 4:5

My office is on the 7th floor of a 15 story building. On any given day I find myself having elevator conversations with random people. All I need is a moment of eye contact and I will engage with anyone from the building custodians to the state commissioner. I do this because I never know if I will have certain opportunities again; therefore I aggressively engage every potential opportunity.

Let's reminisce for a moment. How many "I should've (s)" do you have in your life. How many moments have you let slip away. Who is the young lady that made you say, "I should've asked her out" – or the gas you should've purchased last night before the price went up by 30 cents this morning?

"The King will reply, 'Truly I tell you, whatever you did for one of the least of these brothers and sisters of mine, you did for me' (Matthew 25:40).

Making the most of every moment is not just about what you can get from others. There's more to it than shopping for sales or sticking around long enough to win the raffle. The moments that really count are life-changing. These moments are made when you are too tired to wrestle with your son on the living room floor but you do it anyway because he misses you. They are made when your daughter wants you to read her a story even though it's already past her bedtime. The moments that count mostly includes those moments at the end of your work day, when after mowing the lawn and attending Bible study, your wife desires a little bit of quality time with you – just to talk. Don't take those moments for granted or treat them as burdens.

Do This: Take time to really engage with people by putting down your phones or any other distractions while you are with them. Show them they are important to you by giving them your undivided attention.

Pray This: Heavenly Father, I thank you for the people you have put in my life. I realize that they are here for a reason and so am I. Help me to see your will in every relationship, to fulfill your purpose with every encounter. Let my life be a blessing to my loved ones as well as strangers. In Jesus' name, Amen.

Worthy Challenge Review

1. On a scale of 1 to 5, 1 being the worst and 5 being the best you could do, how well would you rate your success with this week's worthy challenge?

2. What was your biggest hurdle to overcome as it relates to this week's worthy challenge?

3. What did you do to overcome that hurdle?

4. As you continue into the second week of this challenge, what will you do better than you did last week?

5. On a scale of 1 to 5, 1 being utter failure and 5 being total victory, how successful do you believe you will be as you complete this worthy challenge by the end of this week?

Worthy Challenge #22: Give it Your Best Shot

"God has given each of you a gift from his great variety of spiritual gifts. Use them well to serve one another."

1 Peter 4:10

A few years ago my wife and I took my son, Samuel to his first pro football game. Two great teams, the Tennessee Titans and Chicago Bears battled it out. At half-time, the Titans were down and Samuel was convinced we'd lose. I told him, "Keep watching, son. The game's not over." I had to keep reminding him of that whenever the game was not going in favor of the Titans. When the clock ran out – well let's just say it was a long flight back to Chicago.

One of my favorite highlights of that game was when Ahmard Hall hurdled over a defender to avoid a tackle! It reminded me of the first time my brother ran the high hurdles in high school. Our entire family went to see him compete. He started the race strong and we were sure he'd win. Until he hit the 1st hurdle...and the 2nd...and the 3rd...knocking each of them flat. My family's not known for our sympathy and so it didn't take long for everyone to start laughing. But my brother kept running; bruising his shins and scarring his ankles as he hit hurdle after hurdle. People can say whatever they want about that race, but on that day no one could ever call him a quitter. Even though he was sure to lose, my brother gave it his best. By his senior year in high school his was arguably one of the best hurdlers in all of Kentucky and that brought credit upon himself and the school he ran for.

What gifts and abilities has God given you? You may not be a star athlete or a great singer but you have a gift. Read what Paul says about it:

"If your gift is to encourage others, be encouraging. If it is giving, give generously. If God has given you leadership ability, take the responsibility seriously. And if you have a gift for showing kindness to others, do it gladly" (Romans 12:8).

Do This: This worthy challenge is about accepting your God given gift and doing your best with it. Whatever God has gifted you to do, decide now to use it in service to others. Make it a point to exercise your gift this week to be a blessing to a neighbor, stranger, or whomever God places in your path.

Pray this: Heavenly Father I thank you for the gifts and abilities that you have entrusted me with. Today, I have decided to never hold back. Provide opportunities for me to glorify your name as I operate under the guidance of your Holy Spirit. In Jesus' name I pray, Amen!

Worthy Challenge Review

1. On a scale of 1 to 5, 1 being the worst and 5 being the best you could do, how well would you rate your success with this week's worthy challenge?

2. What was your biggest hurdle to overcome as it relates to this week's worthy challenge?

3. What did you do to overcome that hurdle?

4. As you continue into the second week of this challenge, what will you do better than you did last week?

5. On a scale of 1 to 5, 1 being utter failure and 5 being total victory, how successful do you believe you will be as you complete this worthy challenge by the end of this week?

Worthy Challenge #23: Be a Better Man Today Than You Were Yesterday

"Not that I have already obtained all this, or have already arrived at my goal, but I press on to take hold of that for which Christ Jesus took hold of me"

Philippians 3:12

Great men are often their own toughest critics. They are the ones who reflect on a victory and still manage to think of several things they will do better on the next go around. These men are found reading books instead of watching sit-coms. You find them locking the building doors when everyone else has already gone home. Ask them for twenty and they'll give twenty-one. For these men, being good is simply not enough. They want "great". They strive for perfection!

Recently a sport's drink commercial caught my attention with the slogan, "One More". The commercial showed footage of coaches and athletes training in preparation for a football game. The commercial is inspiring as they work through their fatigue; faces drenched in sweat as they run drills on dusty grounds into the sunset and push heavy weights to their max. Printed on the ceiling over the weight-bench is their mantra, "ONE MORE" in bold capital letters. As these young warriors head to the field with confidence the screen fades to black leaving the words "WIN FROM WITHIN" noticeably across the screen. That commercial is so powerful that I wish I had thought of it!

"But he said to me, "My grace is sufficient for you, for my power is made perfect in weakness." Therefore I will boast all the more gladly about my weaknesses, so that Christ's power may rest on me" (1 Corinthians 12:9).

The challenges you face were not meant for you to bear alone. That is precisely the reason why The Comforter was sent from heaven to earth. This worthy challenge intends to challenge you to invite the Holy Spirit that abides inside of you to play an active role in your life. Then, and only then will you have the power to be a better man today than you were yesterday.

Do This: Each night before bed, reflect on your day and ask God to forgive you in areas where you fell short. Wake up the next morning with an attitude that says, "I will be a better man today!"

Pray This: Holy Spirit, go with me today. Guide my steps and light my path. Show me the best things to do and the best things to say in every situation. Help me to be a better man. In Jesus' name, Amen!

Worthy Challenge Review

1. On a scale of 1 to 5, 1 being the worst and 5 being the best you could do, how well would you rate your success with this week's worthy challenge?

2. What was your biggest hurdle to overcome as it relates to this week's worthy challenge?

3. What did you do to overcome that hurdle?

4. As you continue into the second week of this challenge, what will you do better than you did last week?

5. On a scale of 1 to 5, 1 being utter failure and 5 being total victory, how successful do you believe you will be as you complete this worthy challenge by the end of this week?

Worthy Challenge #24: Finish Strong

"But I do not account my life of any value nor as precious to myself, if only I may finish my course and the ministry that I received from the Lord Jesus, to testify to the gospel of the grace of God"

Acts 20:24

If you are reading this chapter I pray it is not because you skipped ahead, but because you have been dedicated enough to take on each worthy challenge with your best foot forward! If so, you should be proud of yourself. If you have taken the challenge with a close friend or a small group, now is a good time to share fist bumps, high-5's or whatever it is you do to say "Well done" to each other. In fact, throw a pizza party, hit the golf course, or just relax. But don't relax too long. There's still a lot more of the race to run.

As we celebrate yesterday's success, we still understand that there is a future. In the future, problems will arise. In the future, we will be tempted to go back to our old ways – to do things the way we did them before we became Iron Men and God Chasers. Now is the time to serve notice to the devil and his imps that we will not bow! Jeffery Arnold knows the power of brothers in Christ who work together towards a better tomorrow. He writes, "The common bond that links Christians together is not the similarity of our past, but the convergence of our future."[5] I believe you want the story at the end of your life to be like that of the apostle Paul who wrote:

"I have fought the good fight, I have finished the race, I have kept the faith" 2 Timothy 4:7

I gave up wrestling my senior year in high school because I was transferred to a school that I did not like. There are times when I regret that decision because I think of what could have been. I could have won the state championship. I could have earned a scholarship. I could have done a lot of things. The harsh reality is that I failed to finish strong and therefore I will never know what "could have

---

[5] Jeffrey Arnold, The Big Book on Small Groups. (Downers Grove: InterVarsity Press, 2004) 87.

been". Don't let this be your testimony. Live your Christian life with no regrets. You have begun well. Now finish; finish strong!

Do This: Identify a friend or a group of friends who you know could benefit from this book. Buy them a copy and ask them to join you over the next couple of months as you start your annual worthy challenges. Commit to meeting with them once a week. Pray with them and encourage them in the spirit of mutual respect and accountability.

Pray This: Thank you, God for helping me to finish strong. Because of the power of the Holy Spirit I was able to make it through this year of worthy challenges. Strengthen me as I prepare to enter a new year as a better son, husband, father, brother, uncle, and most of all; a disciple of Jesus Christ. Your love for us has made us who we are. We are Iron Men and God Chasers! In Jesus' name, Amen!

Worthy Challenge Review

1. On a scale of 1 to 5, 1 being the worst and 5 being the best you could do, how well would you rate your success with this week's worthy challenge?

2. What was your biggest hurdle to overcome as it relates to this week's worthy challenge?

3. What did you do to overcome that hurdle?

4. As you continue into the second week of this challenge, what will you do better than you did last week?

5. On a scale of 1 to 5, 1 being utter failure and 5 being total victory, how successful do you believe you will be as you complete this worthy challenge by the end of this week?

Bibliography

Arnold, Jeffrey. *The Big Book on Small Groups.* (Downers Grove: InterVarsity Press, 2004.

Barna Group. *Reading Habits of Today's Pastors.* n.d. . https://www.barna.org/barna-update/congregations/613-reading-habits-of-today-s-pastors (accessed September 17, 2013).

Steven R. Covey, The 7 Habits of Highly effective People. New York: Free Press. 2004.

Gangle, Kenneth O. *Team Leadership In Christian Ministry.* Chicago: Moody Publishers, 1997.

Scott, Elizabeth. *The Stress Management and Health Benefits of Laughter.* n.d. http://stress.about.com/od/stresshealth/a/laughter.htm (accessed September 19, 2013).

All scripture references are derived from various translations of text available on www.blueletterbible.org

Visit www.c4ministries.com for more information about the author.

ABOUT THE AUTHOR

Corey D. Sturdivant is a third generation military veteran and graduate from Liberty Baptist Theological Seminary who is dedicated to making disciples for Jesus Christ. Sturdivant is the founder and Senior Pastor of Champions Christian Community Church in Henderson, CO. Their vision is to make Jesus famous and they strive to do this in three ways:

1. Honor God through Worship

2. Humble Selves through Prayer

3. Help Others through Service

Sturdivant is passionate about discipleship and believes his purpose is to help men discover their roles in marriage and family. He has been married to his beautiful wife, Jennifer since 2000 and they have two fantastic children.